Firewalk

Firewalk

Poems by Katherine Bitney

TURNSTONE PRESS

Firewalk
copyright © Katherine Bitney 2012

Turnstone Press
Artspace Building
206-100 Arthur Street
Winnipeg, MB
R3B 1H3 Canada
www.TurnstonePress.com

Turnstone Press gratefully acknowledges the assistance of the Canada
Council for the Arts, the Manitoba Arts Council, the Government of
Canada through the Canada Book Fund, and the Province of Manitoba
through the Book Publishing Tax Credit and the Book Publisher
Marketing Assistance Program.

Some of these poems have been previously published in slightly different
form. "The Skate," "Just Past Lammas," and "Ski Jumpers" (published as
"The Aerialists") appeared in *Contemporary Verse 2*. "More," Coming to
Solstice", and "Kite" appeared in *Prairie Fire*. "More" was broadcast on
CBC Radio.

Printed and bound in Canada by Friesens for Turnstone Press.

Library and Archives Canada Cataloguing in Publication

Bitney, Katherine
    Firewalk / Katherine Bitney.

Poems.

ISBN 978-0-88801-406-1

    I. Title.

PS8553.I8776F47 2012   C811'.54   C2012-905389-9

To the Messenger at the Ancestor Gates

Thanks to:

Dennis Cooley, my editor
Andris Taskans for your help and insight
Michelle Forrest for taking the time

Contents

Hands Catch Fire

Firewalk

You Cannot Rest

A Spell Against Being Cursed

Whosoever has laid a curse on me   Take it back
Whosoever has laid a curse on me   I break it

I send you back the shards
I send you back the pieces
I send you back the broken spell

Look to the Left

Look to the left, where the past comes in, where you are
followed, the shoulder you look over when you walk at night,
down dangerous streets. Salt thrown over the left shoulder, this
way you are dogged, followed.

Left is where the past leaves its clues, money in the pocket,
a hand out receiving. Coins from an old leather bag, black
rimmed. Its raised images: owls, insignia of a king. Drachma.
Penny. Coins of the realm, and who ruled. Coins on the eyes of
the dead to pay the ferryman.

Coins in the arsenal of magic, pentacles, the middle world,
manifesting. Coins emptied onto the left hand. A door open on
one of them. Too small to go through.

Left is the shoulder you look over to see what is following you.
Left is the hand that receives. Takes in. Calls home. Put the
coins in the pocket of the past to look at later.
The past jingling in your pocket.

Look to the left, your hand, your heart, your shoulder, watch
your left back, what comes up behind you comes up there. Left
because you left it in the past. Door closed, too small to get
through. Your giant head looking into a dollhouse.

Retreat says the prairie dog. Hang says the bat.

Fist

Your anger is a fist. No, a fire
in the voice box. Burns up words in your throat.
Your heart is a fist, muscle and veins,
arteries, twisting. Fist of a life,
opening. Four chambers, four lives.
Four parts of a song. Flight of bird in one,
lope of wolverine in another. Embryo, singer, stranger.
Fish. Foetus. Rivers, hair. Mouth
the line of a long-walked path.
Face, a map of the worlds.

You are hunting a mirror for that face of a rage
still burning like a bog fire in the forest of your past.
What you see: astonishment. Hair in flames.
Nose and eyes askew. A snake crawling
down your forehead, your hands of striking. Look back,
your path is burning behind you.

Don't imagine this dance is ever done,
your cells releasing memes like sweat from their skin,
it's never done. Your bones seek their homes in your sockets,
muscles ache to run, put arms into the shape of wings.
You would be free, you say, so keep dancing.
How tightly you were wrapped in those sleeves of need,
those needs not yours, I swear. It's unwrapping
the bound feet of old women, crumpled bones
and dead flesh. What is left,
you will dance on anyway.

So let me dance you through this then. Let me harp
or sing or drum for you. Expect sore soles,
swollen knees, an aching back, locked hips.
Expect arms numb, fingers ablaze with blood
rushing through. See,
the mazurka of your soul returning.

November

You won't get me out there. I'm talking to you. Too cold. Too much wind and I always hate wind. It reminds me of you. The window closed and the curtains flopping against it. Frost on the pane.

Snow everywhere. A skating rink in the garden. The radio deep into the night. Light on. You are afraid.

And the north sky out beyond the curtains the window all the stars of time and the darkness of the North. Where is there to go?

The dog is watching. He curls in front of the furnace, where it's warm. Twitches in his sleep. Looks up.

I'm talking to you. Here's what I want to say. It was cold and the nights were dark and
windy. I'm talking to you.

The Skate

where earth meets sky, that's where the blades go down.
hit ice. no language for this, the loops,
the steel against ice. feet of a child in the clean white boots.
mind on the business of glide and push.

this road leads into sky,
air paths zambonied by frost.
rise up, skater, and zoom the roads.
the breathing of spirits makes air fill with hope.
scrape and drag of blades,
snow puffs and blue blue sky, the roads to take.

how holy it is. you can skate to heaven.
hills dusted with snow. sharp in-and-
out breath of a child.

when you are six and in love with the body
who will tell you no?

You Cannot Rest

You cannot rest in those arms, they are not god's,
they are not the arms of the universe. You cannot rest in them.
Do not be fooled. Do not be called away,
do not let the voices speak. Say you hear there is rest,
an answer. Do not listen to the call, don't go.
You cannot rest in those arms. Not there.
They will sing to you, and the beat is the beat of your heart,
your hips swaying, the turning side to side of your mind.
We know, we know, child, and you are not one. No child.
You cannot rest, no, can't speak what they want to hear.

And seeing the snow, the low light, you want to go home,
you want to go home. Seeing the gravestones,
you want to go home. Can't sing enough
into the cold, the stillness, can't sing enough
into the low light, the ball of sun hanging
in the south, between the trees.

Living on Tiptoe

So much in my head I stopped reading. There was too much in my head I stopped listening stopped hearing looking.

There was too much. In my head I stopped. Hearing too much too much listening looking. There was too much.

In my head too much listening too much seeing too much.

There was too much in my head. I stopped. Listening hearing looking I stopped reading. Stopped.

Now listen I stopped hearing I stopped looking. I ought to have known. I ought to have stopped. I ought to have not been. There.

Now you can see. There was too much.

I should have known. I should have known. I should have known.

The Maidens All in Green

They grow their bodies like vines,
long hair a rolling sea.
Forest of green girls, singing.

I should be the crone along the road
but I'm a girl with a limping heart.

All green and fair.
They are maidens at the well.
Priestesses calling up the dawn,

Watch, O maidens,
among you walks a girl
pulling out her hair,
herding her family,
shepherding.

Leaving

I am not allowed in the house any more. I should be anguished but the Raven that I am snaps her beak and closes an exit on the moment of my death. I am gone from the house as I wished and a wind sweeps through with me in its wings. Oh the voices of my children, the cries and the sleeping, every moment of it moving through the house. Who am I? Who were we?

They have called in the Crones of the night. Brought down the great dragons. Cerridwen flew in on the wind. With their brooms and their fire they have cleared me away. They have burned all my spells to the ground.

The Sun at Midwinter

You were there. I saw you. Notwithstanding the clouds. Fog.
I saw you through the circle of stones,
the lintels clear and square against earth. Somehow,
we unbound them, laid them in a line. Made sentences of them,
let the story ramble on. We unbind it still
and that was the risk, always.

A Foetus May Linger

A foetus may linger and wish not to leave.
Its spirit wanting to go back, to leave the flesh where it is,
fly home before it loves the body, loves the world.
Before its desire is survival, the journey
in that moment just before birth.

The Girl in the Garden

When the girl walked in the garden again I feared I might meet
her, with her iris her iris in her hand. I hear you, you wraith
of a twisted time. How could I know why you left your body
unformed. Why didn't you finish it, why did you say no. Why
do you pace the garden year on year, swept away. I feared to
find your grave, never saw your small white coffin. Know it
only from a dream.

When the dead walk your garden you must offer them food
and drink. But what will you drink, Iris Girl? White wine?
Lemonade? Your mother has made cookies and put out some
fruit. Will you have them? Will you turn away twirling your
parasol?

The Black Lacquer Dream

I am painting cranes and chrysanthemums like the Chinese, black and gold, the flowers pink, and a nightingale on a twig.

I dream this: the easel in the morning room, black lacquer to hand, the brushes ready, oils squeezed on the palette. I could sit for hours dreaming this: the chair, the birds, the flowers and the light in from the dawn. It doesn't matter. I am dreaming at last. I am dreaming at last. The strokes are almost in my hand, the smell of paint in my nose, on my tongue. The floor pushes up on the bones of my feet, calls down the instep. Just age. My hands covered with silver rings and body still in a nightgown. The chair almost there with the window behind it and a white horse somewhere to pasture. Each time I return the call is still here, the movement of spirits in stones, the scurry of rodents under the grass.

Call Lizard

Who dreams on the rocks in the sun. He dreams
what he will or will not choose.
Lizard turns, face up, tongue tasting. Two voices,
two spirits. Or more. What he knows: how to dream it.
There is no language for this
crossing of time and belief and no trail back.
Not even the right words.

The poet is lost in the thicket. Pricking her hands.
Cold roses, old trees, no words among them.
How do you call her back from the poisons
in her hands? She supplicates
then lowers them. What is next to you, write that.
Mist from the river. Touch me.
Don't touch me.

I Am Cold

I am cold from the ghost inside,
she moves around the house of my body,
room to room, leaves her shoes
in the doorways, shawls flung on the chairs.
We are two spirits nodding as we pass.
One cannot speak to the other. One wants to speak.
Is that her moving in my skin?
She will not make me die and ghost with her.
Speak again, or speak for the first time, ghost.
Speak to, not through, me.

I want to take to my bed and dream.
Like the dead girl, dream.

Black Dragon Eggs

I rest a crystal ball on the podium of my palms. It pulls me in,
eyes first, as a shark pulls in a seal. Now look what I've done,
called up, in the hard eye of my mind.

Black dragon watches three eggs, not his, not his. Try to catch him
and he morphs the light, not me. Not me. Bends light
in his hiding. A black wisp. And all that is left is the skeleton
of a fish. And now he is a fox, pretty as foxes always are.
You think it's you, says he.
Your heart burns, your hair is on fire.

He may be a guardian, the eggs may be your souls.
You may have mistaken him for a thief. You think that it's you.
A fox, a ripple in the light.

Dancing the Past

This is the dance I am doing, a life held in the bones,
and time means nothing. You move your mind aside
and the drum calls up shocks,
breathlessness. You hang like a rag
on a holy tree. Motionless
except for the idle swing of your arms.
You dangle over the land, a man hanged.
Shoulders holding it all. You try not to die.
All else, the body, flailing
above earth. Feet not touching.

You cannot take a breath against this.
Swinging and swinging your bones.

Wolf

You've walked with wolves all your life,
put your hands on their backs in the night,
not seeing their paws on your chest in the morning.
Not feeling their heat, the shape of wolf leg,
not seeing their dog smiles, their dance in the moonlight,
your bed a wide field in the stars, and there they sing to you,
to the sky,
and you don't know it.

Don't tell me you missed this in your dreams.

August Evening

Silence except for crows. Is everyone home for dinner?
Is everyone in for the night? Small birds, the cats,
the butterflies, the bees. Late garden.
End of the summer run. All things rest in the night.
Even the trees, not quite sad. At rest. If you ask
they ignore you, and don't. Want to share your evening.
Speak through the window. Blue-green needles reach
for your heart or your arm.

Heard geese again. Early calling. Nights cool
and the sun shorter in the sky. What is dying now.
Gently. The heat and the green.
For heaven's sake, be with me.

Yes, That Was Me

Yes, that was me walking your hills. Me sleeping
on the floor of your forest. And that was me
shadowed against that high full moon. She's wanting now
to wane with the season,
yellow with the leaves.

I was standing between moon and earth, looking
for the doors to the other worlds. Reaching
for a latch, hunting the right rune,
the stones stacked just so.

The Wren in the Empty Church

As though at winter solstice all birds know the church is empty
but the wren. Trapped in the stones, the wrong stones. Looking
for the dark yew trees, somewhere to hide
from the hawk. To watch the sun die,
rise again. Out there, stones in the field, bang of the church bell.
Wren sings in the vaults, against the windows. Trapped.
Not daring to hope for a cold wind under its tiny wings.
The voice knows itself, turning and turning
back from the high walls, the saints.
The voice singing
to itself. To itself.

You Think That It's You

Two Brothers

Two brothers, one with a drum. Two brothers,
one with a bird and one with a drum.
Two brothers. One flies, one dances. One flies,
one dances. One drums, one plays a flute. One sits
with the dead, one opens and closes the doors.
One flies, one swims.
Two brothers, one with a drum.

Drum Dances

Dancing again. Drum spinning. Black bear
on his haunches in the North. In the West
a howling. Owl flies out
from the East. To the South, half circle, half arc. On my head
a swan. Dance between worlds, doors open. What kindness
walks there, one world open to another. Sweeps
the wind through doors,
windows, up streets.

You keep dancing, feet pounding the earth, the floor
of your house, shaking the worlds with it. Keep swaying
and the breezes your arms, your hands make, push the air
out, in, circles, whirlpools, shaping what?
You don't know. Just the heart of you remembering
the steps, the gestures needed.

A door of the heart swings open. Listen,
listen. I'm speaking. Your flesh raging,
bones on fire. A dance wants to hook itself to your drum,
the bone fire, the keening in your cells.

Voice

Voice is the body jigging in its cells.
Voice is the air-raid siren always about to sound.
The horror of its call, its not calling.
Voice is not song but a screaming in the bones.
Cells are all throats, choking.

Voice is not light in the cells, the throat,
not words in the mind, on the tongue blue with truth.
Not struggling behind the teeth to run forth,
voice is not this. Voice is the residue,
the tumble out of what happens,
or doesn't. You lose all breathing, forget,
you float away into it.
On a cushion of sound you lay your head down,
breathe only light. Eyes closed. Someone singing.

What you find in the voice box:
dead birds, dried, old as the body.
A singing and singing against death.

So I am calling for voice in the house of spirits.
Calling in dream, in the hollow of that time,
the empty space between then and now. Look,

I say, I have broken the spells, torn down the walls.
Called back the yes and the heart and the dragon
out of the earth. The one with the blue flowers
on her head. Blue balls of light.

Walking the Wind

Some say this walk is surfing, gliding the air
paths on silver feet. Everyone is a Mercury,
passing each other, waving through the clouds.
Mistaken for angels, the white air taken for wings,
gowns of light.
Some skiing, some flying. Wind lifts up
as a heart rises.
We set our feet on it,
ice and cloud.

Yggdrasil: The World Tree

This tree holds the circles of the worlds
in the hand of its roots. Lower worlds smooth, sure.
The Upper World is ragged, its branches bedraggled crows.
Yet the tree holds the Upper Worlds in its high branches,
and the Middle Worlds out in the last long arms.

Worlds all pale green, growing like early leaves. Always.
Riot of green. Tree grips the worlds
easily in the branches, globes in claws.

Windwalking 1

You think it is you, riding in that wind. That wind
hauling snow into the breaking spring. That wind
hurling snow, bouncing spruce boughs,
shaking the naked rose canes,
skinny fingers of a summer ghost.
You think it is you, and it is, your own breathing
up there and the breeze
of you dancing.

Our Lives in Winter

Snow drifts blue to the earth, sparkling always.
The safety of indoors and the fire. What little there is,
is warm as we want to be. The goddess skis
in the forest, birch lighting her way day and night.
Into the heart of the woods that give her home. Bow
across her back.

Our houses in the blue night, long shadows of the mountains,
trees striping them. Who can sit all day at the windows,
frost on our fingers. But who cannot look. The gods
are clear as stars. Striding the worlds, oblivious of us, and not.
They could crush our roofs with their boots, easy. Business
too big for us in our winter huddle. Quarrels and creation.

What do we know of all this, busy with our own
quarrels in the tight winter quarters.
Not much to do but card wool
and spin, sharpen swords, tell tales
into the night. And sing, sing in the smoky halls.
If a traveller comes by we rejoice. Relief from the boredom
of each other. The stink of the cows and fire.

We watch the wolf on his circuit, his lope around the edge
of our land, watching the house as he goes. He stops, tests the air
with his black nose. Ears up and a question in his eyes.
We might wish it a question of spirit:
are we well, can he teach us?

But his question is land and its game: are there hares?
Are there sheep?
Are there calves?
Are there guns?

Coming to Solstice

This is the sun that belongs to the stag in winter. Pale lemon
light reaches out its arms of promise. What is true.
The ache of your memories and mine. Snow dawdles down
And somewhere in the bush the stag waits. Daily
the sun moves lower, into his antlers.
He knows where to stand, how to seize it
a sunset hooked between trees.

Desire and Doing

I used to run to doing, desire
propelling like a swamp buggy
engine, pulling air, skimming
the bayou. Reeds pushed back
by its force. A wake
that topples gators in its waves.

Or fly, perhaps I flew, as in dreams
one flies, a human body with wings,
sans gêne. Mind hungry. Head
maybe of an owl or an eagle, to and fro,
hunting. Bloodsport of the mind.

How bewildering to not desire, to not hunger.
And want now to run to everything at once.

Leaving the Double

Not the body but its mud, its residue.
Not the residue but the damp imprint.
Not the imprint but the memory of trees, of water.
Not the memory, but the effect.

Not the effect but the twin still standing.
No sorrow for the dead.
For the lost years, rage.
For ashes in the forest.
For the dead who walk the sea.

Strength Crosses Skill: A Tarot Reading

I'm not going to find the answer. Cards provocateurs. Strength
crossing Skill and Sorcery. Who cares? Two days I hunt
for the meaning, fish my brain for a word, a feeling.

Finally the picture: a rocky sandstone gorge, canyon, tall
stones, a cliff, too deep to fathom. Never mind.
Up from that gully seeps water. Rises quickly, fills
the canyon to the brim. Clear water. You can see the canyon
under it but who cares, it overflows the cliffs,
makes a beach of the mesa top.

Somewhere else, near a stream, a stand of trees.
Ferned forest. Green water gushes
from the holes in their sides.

So this is my answer. Strength fills the canyon of heart, feeds
trees to overflowing, roots up.
They are pouring it out. So many of them.

When the Land Enters Your Body

When the land enters your body, birds, stones, the grass
tufted and dry. Sky a mind blue with thought.

You have stood here so long, breathed with the wind,
the smell of the cricket's voice,
the slimy scent of the slough.

The land enters your nose, your mouth, eyes, ears. Touch. How
you stand. And where, how, do you enter desire,
or it you?

Restart the voice, the mind, now mute and back-turned, zipped.
You are part mind entreating itself,
Voice is your hands. All in a centre of fire you dancing,
shouting like a crazy woman.

Calling, calling. Why don't you speak to me?
Gimme back my voice
my juice
my jump and desire.

Well waddya know, Eros drives the universe again,
desire in. Cold fusion. Sun bursting.
A fluffy planet floating on a pond.
Smoky voice at the end of the line.
And who would imagine that the engine in the sun is love.

The Journey

Seems endless this journey, no stopping it. The bus pulls out
again, churns toward the West, to the rolling hills
and the high ground of home. The prairie passing
spring after spring the green fields,
the small towns passing. She's waiting. Arms out.
And a garden of weeds to be cleared.

Arms open, tea on. And her stories told over and over.
In the garden lies buried her wedding ring and the bones
of an unborn child. Her rowans and hawthorns hide spirits
and lies. The fountains drip blood. She is vexed
by the cruelty of magpies and crows. I am weeding again,
the same weeds, same ground. Yarrow gone wild. Comfrey
unchecked. Rhubarb gone dizzily to seed.
Her spells thick as moss on the stones, hanging like grapes
from the trees. She cleans nothing. Retells and reweaves.

No stopping it, not even now she's gone, there is still the bus
and the West. Mist on the road, tractors
pushing up dust in the fields.

The Eagle Dance

Arms ache from holding, seeking the updraft,
covering the air with pinions, the forward crook of the wings.
Riding air. Banking left and right.

You think that it's you, down in the reeds,
the water weeds. Falcon flies over,
drops a feather at your feet.
Falcon flies out of your third eye
and what god was that. What speed, and the sending
faster than an eagle. Tail a rudder in the wind.

You think that it's you, speaking to fire, to water.
Calling to runes in the trees.

Now the salmon knows how to find home, the river,
the ocean a roof, green growing in its eaves.
Or a lime green crocodile's jaws peeling open.
A turtle flies in the ocean. All beings that fly
flew first in the sea.

Free

Turned myself inside out. The wind as god.
I was not weaving it, just listening. Geese overhead.
Some day they might not come and then what?

Sought the falcon. Called, whistled, breathed.
Saw crystal ball as blue again. Listened.
Ringing in the ears. No words. Body listening.

Saw falcon look back. Bird of Horus. Freyja.
Blue spirit people in the trees.

Full as stone, me. Rocks fill up with water.
Trees pour it out from holes in their trunks.

First thing to note is how hard it is to be free.

Waiting for Snow

You're waiting for snow. As if it might never fall, as if
you hadn't lived deep winters, white, each one. Like
you had never seen snow turning,
turning in air, hour by hour. And you knew nothing of north
winds hurling it, hour by hour, against houses, trees, against
you, your stinging face, your gasping mouth, you standing
in a road, a field, hurrying down a street.
As if you were a child from the South Seas.
A desert walker from the Sahara
filled with a wild white longing.

Iris

They say a ghost can't grow, it remains the age it died. It will
appear to you as it was when the person left the body, and
it's the body image that remains, imprinted on the fabric of
the world, the one we inhabit. So you see them, decapitated
queens and suicides hanging by their necks with rope, lovers
just before one goes off to war and the other dies in childbirth.
You see them screaming through the house for a lover, a
child, absolution, a book, a message, a last important meeting
before battle. A last tryst before one of the lovers is banished, a
murder victim, a mother looking for a lost baby.

They say a ghost stands still in space and time, and in anger
or torment of one kind or another. But not Iris. When she
should have been twenty, someone saw her wander through
my mother's garden, age twenty, a young woman with an iris in
her hand.

Iris should have been a foetus. She should have been a
misshapen lump of pink flesh, she should have appeared as a
baby in a box, a baby without a proper head, without a brain.
She should have been long gone and on to the next thing,
whatever that might be, she should have moved. But she was
waiting for her mother to die, and for her sister to need her
again.

Iris didn't behave like other spirits. She grew quietly in the house while the family went about its business. No one imagined she would do that. From the day her body gave itself up and let itself be put in a small white coffin, she determined not to leave her mother. It was a disappointment to her that her mother could not attend her funeral, and was still in hospital recovering from this difficult birth and death. What held Iris to her mother was her mother's extraordinary compassion in letting that body die. Such love she had not dared imagine, but there it was. The body had not come out as she had wished, she had warned her mother in dream that it wasn't going to come out right, but no one listened. So Iris let it grow and hoped against hope that her mother would let it go.

She was there when the father and the two young sisters stood by the graveside as the priest gave the blessing, watching and sorrowing for the girls. From here Iris could see why the body had not come out right, why some deep part of her had balked and decided against coming in as a girl. The father wore sunglasses to disguise his grief. The sisters were angry under their confusion. The mother lay in the hospital sedated and healing up the sutures around the Caesarian that the birth had required.

She called herself Iris, though they had chosen another name for her. Because what should have been a brain in her head was a stem that looked like an iris.

I get emails from Iris sometimes. She sends messages, and sometimes she sent JPEGs. Once, it was a crow showing a tear-shaped diamond. I thought it was meant to be my soul, but it was not, it was the diamond tear of compassion. How could she have known? And once it was the body of a child under a blanket, in the garden, under the soil. I wondered if it meant there was a body in the garden, or if it was a sign that something had died there in a child, not her, she was never a child, not really, but perhaps a child who had lived there, someone beaten to death, or left to starve. Who knows?

And once she sent me a picture of an underground cave, and in it was a butter box with a curled up snaky foetus dreaming of a cartoon self, all blond and curly and smiling like a Barbie doll.

Another time it was an owl, flying down to its own reflection in a pond. I tried to find a photo of this so I could paint it. And sometimes it was a group of drumming shamans, all ribbons and twisting bodies dancing on a steppe. How immense it all must have seemed to them, no cities, no planes. Just the sky and the endless fields of grass. I did not see horses in this picture, though Iris did remind me I had a flying horse I sometimes used to go on journeys.

I wondered why she sent me these pictures. Iris was not meant to be a real girl, but I suppose a spirit can do what it likes. Wander in the garden all grown up, drop books in the middle of the night.

I answer her emails, always, I do not want to drop the thread that binds us, sisters in two worlds.

Bird Dancing

You could say I was a dancer once
knees shimmied the hips like a wader
a snipe or a heron, flamingo shuddering in the sun.

Or a tireless grouse pounding the lek
breast close to the earth its pull the call of hens
and the thump of the world's green heart.

Leks are full of old dances, beat down by the feet of our fathers
three-toed shamans they called all the worlds to this one
for the dance.

Now I dance like a vulture, side to side
knees aching and hips off kilter
no leks no dance floor but the earth around a kill
or the bounce of a treetop in the wind.

And yes I said I am not a dancer, but now look, you
old song of the stones, you call my arms
into water, bones into the slow sway of trees.
Hands catch fire, lungs breathe out
eagles and eagles and eagles.

Odin

Odin came calling. As always, disguised. Who knew he was
under that floppy hat (what man wears a hat anymore?). His
one good eye piercing the dark (but what man wears a patch
anymore?). Who knew those two ravens were his. They were
witches or shamans or birds lost in the winter from hunger,
chased by a murder of crows. Such is the world, Odin says. All
things must work to survive.

Who knew it was him in that hat, in that cloak (and what man
wears a cloak anymore?) Who knew it was him in the bar,
his one good eye on a beer. He turned to the dance floor and
watched with amusement. Men brawling, girls primping, beer
spilt on the floor. Like home, thought Odin. Smiled.

When Odin came calling I wasn't prepared for the rap on the
door (and what man carries a staff anymore?). Who knew
he'd stopped off for a beer? And here's me at the door with my
mouth hanging open, not dressed to meet with a god.

Hands Catch Fire

The Walking Gods

How far do gods walk the white road with their names
and their light   a white falcon   The curved line of earth
the bent rune of its flight   How long is their stride and
how clear is their sight

Do they know the horizon they make with their walk
Do they see their paths in the black swan of night

How long do they walk with their names in their mouths
with their staves full of language   their bells and their drums
with their hair full of spells   and their hands full of bones
How deep is their singing   How long is the rune of their voice

Shamans

Now look. This is an old trade. Voices
of a million poets singing down time,
across tribes and nations, whispering
between worlds, their words rolling back and forth, language
after language after language, carrying messages.
Explaining one world to another. What,
in the name of Odin, do we think poetry is for?

Just Past Lammas

Just past Lammas, grapes turning purple in their arbour
and sunflowers already weighted with seeds. Heads down
for the birds to crack the hulls. Wind says Fall
and isn't August always like this?

So come and talk to me. Sun still warm
and the crows nearly grown. The trees call in their saps,
let the leaves go yellow. Among the plants all contracts
negotiated, border disputes now settled.
So it goes until frost. They give and give.
How necessary is this beauty. No creature lives
without making it. Wasps hunting
in a fresh cut lawn. There is a rune for joy.
Come by here, see.

Cougar

Whisker the ground, the air. Small caves in the earth.
Small cave of the mouth. The skit of a mouse
under leaves. A cub's breath.
The stir of a dog on guard.

When to pounce. Love
for the prey bursts through the blood
and the tail twitches, silent breath.

Glory to the growl and to the scream.

Mermaids

Women of the sea in their mermaid gowns sway as they sing,
mouths open like scallop shells or the snouts of fish breathing.
No. Like sirens on rocks, keening. Eyes shining.
Gold, red, blue, green strapless fishtail gowns cover their mermaid
no-feet. Here they are fish out of water, or should be, but
the orchestra now is their sea.
To whom do they croon the ancient songs?

It's not that we have forgotten them: The pattern of tones, the pitch
of their cries, their open mouths the caves of our memory.
Long ago, they sing, *long ago. Where earth meets sea.* Beached
in their seaweed skins they walk on knives,
remind us. *Long ago. Long ago.*

But whom are they kidding? We know them, the silkies,
the seal women, fish women, calling us out
from their rocks in the waves. We draw near the edge
as we have always done, sing back,
sing back the liturgy of the sea.

Freyja

said follow me, wolves racing with her.
Tip of her staff on fire.

She knocked the earth four times. She turned,
a cougar, a falcon,
an old woman.
Turned three times deosil.
She spoke dark birds, smoke rings,
mountain, truth.

Up the Stones

You move, shadow of hawk hunting, owl
hunting, coming to ground. The claw of fire
in you. Air in you, a river in a sea. Talons out,
you reach for a perch, for prey. Light
in the mind. Light in the space
where a coffin was removed, the egg
put out to air, get light.

Like a shadow or a bird. Hawk hunting, owl hunting,
coming to ground. Their claws of the fire in you. Air
in you, a river in a sea. What to do with this but open,
release. Disperse into atoms of sky, wind.
Talons out, light in the mind. Light
in the space where a coffin was,
the egg put out to air, get light.

Windwalking 2

Here's the thing. You are inside the wind. Summer carries
you within itself. A basket of wind.
You are in the jungles of all worlds,
the gardens gone mad of them. So be it.

Then something snaps, or clicks, the air turns inside out.
You are all power,
no story can contain you. None.
So be it.

How you then become the wind, in summer,
you are the deep full wind
walking. You are the wind,
walking. So be it.

How you become the wind, then, in summer,
you are the deep full wind
walking. You are the wind now,
walking. So be it.

Fall Poem

Raven's back in town. Must be her season, must be
time for her great compassion. Everything leaving, dying,
closing in, autumn folding the rags of summer into frost.
The scent of snow coming. Soon enough,
soon enough, she sings, head feathers ruffed, song all trills
and clonks. Calling with all her heart
from a high tree, its leaves
half eaten by wind.

The Vaulters

Girl meets boy passing over the bull's back   backflips
spinning away one forward   one back   The bull feels
the air spin from their twist and turn   They must not touch but
the air contracts over the arch of his back
It is not for the jump that he lives
nor the touch of their hands on his horns as they leap
What he lives for is the touch
the air between them when they pass over dead centre
where a saddle would go
where the green light of his heart is

On English Bay

I was reading the sea, eyes half closed
against high summer sun. Gulls and pigeons begged
on the beach. Sky grey and mountains blue, five ships
in the bay unharboured. Sailboats, kayaks, yachts,
speedboats. A few swimmers, dogs off leash.

All day on the beach sand hot and purple with clams.
Crows scudding low and hunting.
I was reading the sea all day, the bay open.

Then I see the horizon and there is the join of earth, sea and
sky both blue, and the line between them. All this in the fire
of a cloud. Event horizon, and the blue haze above and below.
Between them a line, and it is gone, it's light between them
now and a ship on the edge of it. As though at the edge of the
world. Small ship sailing. And it is simply there at the edge of
the horizon, dark and small. What is in it and the turning of the
worlds somewhere behind it.

And here as I write my body again, the ship on the blue horizon
blue sky blue sea. A line of pale yellow between and a small ship
not at harbour.

Let it sail then and show us the horizon. Let it sail then and go
on its way to learning. Not lost, perhaps in a doldrum, there is no
wind or little wind for it. But it will sail, will move out.

It may be a junk or a galleon, the stern just the back of it a deck
a junk's deck. And turning I see a mast, as sail not fully out, now
turning. Showing its prow behind the sail, we are behind the sail,
it is turning, moving toward the horizon, not into the sun but
adjacent.

I hear the mast creak in the wind. Breeze on the face. Sun to the
left. Hand to forehead shading eyes. Looking left to the sun. An
island, land, something we are moving toward, a dark line on the
right horizon.

So we turn our eyes to the right and the land, dark on the sea,
and rising. Will we land or will we sail by it? Going somewhere,
but where. Sail is cream-coloured canvas. Cannot see the
wheel or the steerage. Ripples of the sea around the prow as we
move through it. Light dancing on the water. Dolphins coming
alongside. Hear the wash of the water as they sail it, as we do.
And there is an eagle above, and

is he guiding us past or to his island? There he is and the dolphins
around us. Grey in the blue water.

So the wind is up. We are skimming. Moving with the sun to our
left. Going northwest? The boat is planked, a curved-up stern. Do
not see the prow, it is behind. So we can see trees on the shoreline,
this island, a beach now, we will need to sail past, or anchor
soon. Water clear, sand almost white, and white stones, even the
dolphins are becoming white.

We hit land. Can see the white sand under the water. Ship is still. Somebody has gotten out of the boat and is splashing toward land, shouting. Waving arms. Delight in the water and the white sand. Oh. And going to shore, a figure almost dancing in the sea, running to shore.

We are looking now toward the island, and not to our left, but I see that the sun is still white hot on the horizon. Turn again to the island, and someone has reached shore, pulling the water up to him, bending a bit. It is warm enough to dry without shivering. Someone is on their back on the sand smiling up at the sun and arms and legs spread-eagled on the sand, soft and fine.

There Is a Good Wind

There is a good wind and again somewhere I'm sleeping in it. Small birds sing in the hedges, hidden. Sing for love. The merlins claim a high tree. Wind soughing. Evergreen arms crawl it, swimming the wind. Same wind as sighs in the forest calls the new leaves out, calls out the reeds in the river. Wasps already hunting. Wings against the wind. Crows call, riding it. Gulls riding. Winds of shaping, winds of calling.

When you sleep in wind you are between two worlds. Home, home. All things are possible. Insects open themselves like leaves unfolding. You stand and the blue wind carries you. You walk up its banks, stairs, its cushions, its ladders, its waves, you surf. You sleep in its arms. It sings, speaks to you, voices, voices you know better than your own. Skin of the wind, walker of winds, sleeper in wind.

Grape sap glistens, drips. Birds, the small ones, heard, not seen. Walk the wind. Somewhere in the trees their calling and their trysts. Does someone wish me ill?

You come out alive. Birds fly into the hedge. So while you lie in the wind remembering, remember this fight. Remember this, the day you were born, who sees it.

Fire. Fire, and the body burning.

When One Person Speaks the Truth

When one person speaks the truth, knots untie themselves,
threads fall in coils to the ground. Jars break,
windows blow open, glass flies everywhere. Be careful
where you walk, where you step when one
person speaks the truth.

But since you ask, yes, we have walked hard roads, all of us,
this is the way the walking goes. You leave behind
untied knots, white space, shucked ghosts, old coats
of the mind, the spirit. Debris of language
not your own.

Being clean of it, walk forward.
Walk.

More

This is my thesis Everything's in love What tipped me off was
the universe The rush of galaxies toward each other panting
arms out spinning And the black holes at their cores Hearts
pulling in love Light thumping Matter flinging out like the
tail of a jellyfish like ivy down a wall The love-crazed galaxies
create little star nurseries egg clusters dangling in the deep
What you can say of love is all this *Amor eros manmathah*
From love comes desire From desire comes the world From
the world comes the dynamo of more more more

From more comes infinity from infinity form What tipped me
off was the snag-toothed fish of the deep deep sea You can see
clear to their minds through their dinnerplate eyes where the
questions are written How to live under pressure How to eat
How to test out the shapes How to structure the bones How
to program the genes for the making of form

From form comes desire from desire comes love from love
comes sacrifice from sacrifice more From more comes death
from death comes room for more More More For love is
a dynamo that wants to risk all From risk comes possibility
from possibility comes form From form comes experience
comes wisdom comes joy From joy comes desire from desire
comes love from love comes experience from experience
knowledge from knowledge comes the longing to know more
more more

From desire comes creation from creation joy from joy comes
the moment from the moment comes time from time comes
urgency from urgency *frisson* from *frisson* comes desire to
do more more more What tipped me off was the love talk
of quanta Let's dance And they do   More more For there's
yearning between particle and antiparticle Their love changes
all You can feel in your bones the *frisson* of their touch   your
flesh drives you on to do more more more They do it in the
skies they do it in the sea they do it in deep space where the
galaxies collide You think that's just gravity Uh uh They're in
love And from love comes desire to do more more more

From desire comes action from action comes knowledge and
from knowledge comes the wish to risk more more more
From more comes death from death comes change and from
change comes the moment and the craving for more From
death comes the world   From the world comes desire from
desire comes bodies from bodies comes hunger from hunger
comes action from action comes death What tipped me off
was the whirl of krill the jubilant run of river to sea I know
this from bugs I know this from herons Because rain swoons
down to its sweetheart earth They are all crazy in love They
want more

more more   Nothing is afraid of the little death   Just you   Let's
say you're at the bar and the band is swinging and you see a
star girl a star boy hair spinning   Tell me you don't feel the
heat you want to crash in limbs flailing   Don't panic the
world wants love it wants more more more   What tipped me
off was the jellyfish their liana tails swaying in the difficult sea
they are parasols pulsing their galaxy hearts naked as glass
in the long deep water   What tipped me off was the heat vent
worms slipping in and out of their crimson sheaths looking for
food   for love in the dark for more   For more

And see how your heart now is called to the work   Your body
heats up   Your arms reach out the fire too big to refuse   You
think it's just lust but believe you me   When galaxies mate
their zeal is for love and from love comes desire from desire
comes yearning for knowledge of love   From the knowledge
comes love from love comes sacrifice from sacrifice form
From form comes thought from thought comes speech from
speech comes change comes more more more

Say it now You want more You are abashed by the stuff of
your body   You are shamed by its hunger   You beat back the
pull toward death and desire   You say that the fishes and the
stars have no wishes   Yet they fill up the nebulae with eggs
of light yet they yield up their bodies to make more to make
more   From bodies comes death and from death comes more
comes more comes more comes more

Kite

Last time I was a bird I was a kite. Listen to this. I flew on the
air. It was cushions. Wings out and soft breast pushed against
thermals. I looked down mountains to the plains. I saw the sea,
its rippling fish and the whales piledriving to the dark and the
currents flush with krill. I saw them disappear and rise again
like the gods they are. *Gaude*

And I saw the animals of earth look up and hunt for rain. How
well they know the smell of clouds is the smell of green to
come and they follow. I saw how the land rises, falls, the mice
deep in the grass below. Oh how they run when they see my
shadow pass. *Gaude, Gaude*

When kite flies over, her shadow flicks the grass, green as it
is and sheltering life from the likes of me. If it moves I kill it.
Gaude

Ski Jumpers

Spin on the tip of the wind. Hang trapezing. What
are they thinking in the high air? One-pointed desire
for gold and the twist that makes the deal.
Scribing runes on the sky. Body as knife. As axe.

The jumpers lean forward, arrows pointing to the horizon.
Whistle of wind and snow
beneath them. Earth rises to meet
the lifted staves of them.

Skiers travel the paths between worlds. Earth and sky. Speed
and keep balance. Runemasters, then,
 on skis, snowboards, skates.

They land where earth meets air. Everything
on the opening door of ice.

You Listen

You listen and listen, no words, just a high long note
not wailed, not sung. Someone at your side or nearby.
You don't know who is walking
who are your fellow travellers.

There is more to know, always. Open memory and call.
Earth holds it, water carries it, fire burns away what isn't so,
wind blows the chaff.

Walk Down Drumming

Can't remember my dreams again, just dreaming. Moving inward, nights longer. We go walking together in that world, drumming and singing, weaving up strands of light, drums spinning, into the hills, by the rivers, and in the houses of sleep.

You will dream by day, too, a catnap, say, and there are your ghosts dancing to a mariachi band. A lost child takes your hand and spins you. Guitars thrumming your feet crazy, trumpet driving gold noise through your dream bodies. Streamers spidering around you, little dancers. It could be anything like that.

They want to speak, those voices. Spirits calling, crystal against crystal in the world's core. Calling from the roots of sleeping trees as they walk down, voices like wood, like soil. Calling up from the beds of rivers, from lakes bedding down in ice. Deep currents of matter, measured. Slow as the speech of stones. Been listening. Ear turned, head pitched sideways to hear. Old voices that boom like drums. Don't ask me what they say. You would have to be a drummer.

Seven Crows

In the night I arose and unbaptized myself,
saw seven crows, one lame in the wing.
Did they bring law with them,
black and calling?

I Have No Holy Land

I have no holy land, no city, no Jerusalem, no Mecca.
I have no heart elsewhere, no roots in another place.
No temple to weep at, regret, wish for again,
no stone to circumambulate.

There is only the land I live on. Holy like any other.
The sea, forest, plains, the cities I have lived in, riverine.
As holy as that. Towns on water.
You pray there as you pray at a wall, a stone,
your prayer carries as well as smoke.
Or calls from a tower. Who hears them?
The words dissolve into air, water.
Transform by fire into smoke. What the old shamans knew.
What fed them too, the scent of meat burning.
Wine poured. Pure water.

Everything Complete

Everything complete, folding in. Summer gone, house empty
again. Here comes desire to enter the wind, ride it as it moves
through, tossing trees. A deep sky, no stars, swift journey
of clouds, rattle of rain. The child breathes quietly
in her sleep, dreaming her child dreams, and I will miss her
in the morning and in the evening rising and going to bed.
Oh thank the gods for the eternal now.

Rosebush banging on the rain spout, night wind.
What has this summer been, all gathered
safely in when the family sleeps?
Geese begin to practice their vees, their night flying.
The elements enter me, or I them:
Wind, water, earth, and the great leap of fire.